Ana Alyce Pereira Saraiva

The Birth of Contradiction in Greece

Ana Alyce Pereira Saraiva

The Birth of Contradiction in Greece

An analysis of Antiphon's tetralogies and Plato's Euthymides

ScienciaScripts

Imprint

Any brand names and product names mentioned in this book are subject to trademark, brand or patent protection and are trademarks or registered trademarks of their respective holders. The use of brand names, product names, common names, trade names, product descriptions etc. even without a particular marking in this work is in no way to be construed to mean that such names may be regarded as unrestricted in respect of trademark and brand protection legislation and could thus be used by anyone.

Cover image: www.ingimage.com

This book is a translation from the original published under ISBN 978-613-9-61796-8.

Publisher:
Sciencia Scripts
is a trademark of
Dodo Books Indian Ocean Ltd. and OmniScriptum S.R.L publishing group

120 High Road, East Finchley, London, N2 9ED, United Kingdom
Str. Armeneasca 28/1, office 1, Chisinau MD-2012, Republic of Moldova, Europe
Printed at: see last page
ISBN: 978-620-7-70034-9

SUMMARY

THANKS

No duty is more important than gratitude.

I thank God for accompanying me at all times.

I would especially like to thank Professor Diogo Norberto Mesti da Silva, for watering the great good that is wisdom, giving me so much of his precious time and generously sharing his books and readings with me and enriching our research through his questions. Thank you for sharing your beautiful art with me.

For their constant support and love, I thank my parents, because without the education they gave me, I would be nothing.

I am grateful to my brother for his complicity and advice.

I'd like to thank Heitor, who was with me when I needed him most.

To my dear friends and cousins who live in my heart, thank you for your daily smiles.

And those who are no longer present on the physical plane are special in every memory.

Finally, I would like to thank everyone who has been part of this journey in any way.

SUMMARY

This work aims to discover how the concept of Contradiction arose in ancient Greece and how this phenomenon acted, through an analysis of the works *Testimonies, Fragments, Speeches by* the sophist Antiphon and *Euthyme* by the philosopher Plato. Contradiction is a phenomenon that is difficult to appreciate, but the ability of contradiction to develop new and opposing ideas in people's minds due to the incompatibility found in the same fact has instilled a desire to explore this phenomenon. Thus, the aim of this research is to expand our mode of interpretation by analyzing the dialogues between Antiphon and Plato, with a view to tackling this arduous task of conceptualizing contradiction. In the search for this concept, the study of the sophists and their methods became essential, along with Plato's criticisms of the sophists. From the perspective outlined here, I believe that the examination of conflicting discourses between two theses presented in a plausible and concrete way, which have elements in common and also dissonant, will be extremely important for a satisfactory conclusion regarding the practice of discourses considered to be contradictory and how to interpret them.

Keywords: Contradiction; Discourses; Antiphon; Dialogues; Plato.

INTRODUCTION

This book portrays the incessant search for the birth of a concept, and it is not a question of thinking of it as something absolute. This is because of the historical limits of interpretation, since we are talking about the birth of a concept in the texts to which we have access. Therefore, we limit our field of research to the texts we examine, in order to find the best concept that fits this crucial phenomenon for the birth of the *polis*, philosophy and Greek rhetoric, which is Contradiction. Therefore, the study of contradiction in different scenarios aims to remove this phenomenon from its abstract plane in order to better understand its way of acting and its influence over time in different scenarios.

Since contradiction is a phenomenon that is difficult to perceive and not something tangible and easy to conceptualize, it becomes a great challenge to study. However, it is necessary to analyze this disagreement between words and actions in order to make a correct and plausible decision, whether legal or not; because of this, this research aims to demonstrate how inconsistencies are able to create different forms of interpretation, and a thorough approach to this important topic is necessary.

Given the logical incompatibility between two or more propositions, this allows for an expanded view of different positions, providing the opportunity to create a chain of ideas that demonstrate how divergent opinions build opinions free of prejudices and self-concepts, thus creating distinct conclusions that fit together.

Throughout this book, we will see two different ways of using contradiction, in Antiphon of Athens, whose work deals with legal rhetoric and is the matrix of various reflections, being one of the oldest literary records; together with the work *Euthymedeus* by the great philosopher Plato. As different as they are from each other, the former being known as a sophist and the latter as a great thinker who held premises contrary to those of the sophists, we will draw the essential fuel for our study from the differences and similarities.

In particular, the attempt to arrive at answers before a detailed study is unsatisfactory. In this sense, in Chapter I, it will be necessary to delve into the cradle of this phenomenon, by analyzing contradiction in Greece together with a historical approach to the Sophist movement and the particularities of these thinkers. Chapter II deals with the work of the sophist Antiphon, in which he demonstrates his ability to contradict himself, plus his *Tetralogies,* which show a unique episode of clashes between the accusation and the defense, contemplating the phenomenon of contradiction in various facets. Chapter III looks at other ways of contradicting and educating from the point of view of Plato's *Euthydemus,* in which the game, the struggle and the discourse involving the Platonists and the Sophists will be analyzed, in a journey of confrontations between Plato's dialectic and Antiphon's serious eristics. In this chapter, another point that draws attention is the stance of Socrates, who develops memorable speeches in the debates against the Sophist brothers.

In this concise introduction, I am reinforcing the attempt to deal with the concept of contradiction through the analysis of these very praiseworthy works, which, through their detailed study, allow the reader to draw this very important phenomenon from between the lines.

Hypothetically, we have drawn up an organizational chart which represents some of the elements of contradiction in the dialogues analyzed and which will serve to summarize the problem of contradiction. When analyzing something that is difficult to perceive, it becomes clearer through a diagram how this phenomenon acts, so, depending on the works analyzed, this flowchart was created in order to better synthesize this idea.

<u>ORGANOGRAM</u>

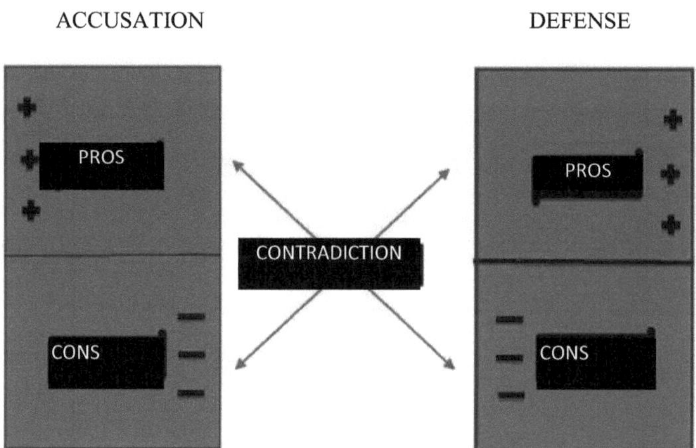

(**−**) → It indicates the devaluation of any argument that challenges the veracity and demonstrates negative aspects that link the subject's conduct to the fact under analysis, compromising it and linking its action (causal link) to the illegal act.

(**+**) → It demonstrates the overvaluation of the arguments that prove the innocence and non-guilt of the subject; in other words, the subject gives extreme value to his version of the facts in order to prove that his view is the correct one and the one that should be adopted by the jurors involved.

PROS → They are the favorable arguments used in favor of one of the sides, so they are ideas organized in a structure that aims to bring together all the possible arguments that will benefit the interested party.

CONS → It portrays the arguments that have the power to incriminate, in order to highlight the negative points that prove guilt, emphasizing everything harmful and counterproductive that could harm those involved.

CONTRADICTION → The contradiction is the inversion, i.e. the transposition between the different arguments.

Based on the drawing, we can see that on one side we have the accusation and on the other the defense, based on the *tetralogies* described in the work of the sophist Antiphon, there is a direct clash between these two poles, with both speeches being narrated in a unique way in his work *Testimonies, Fragments, Speeches*. As we can see, from a confrontation between accusation *and* defense, we have in this interplay the phenomenon of contradiction, which arises between the gaps and incompatibilities of one and the other argument dealt with and suddenly makes an inversion in our thoughts. We are also clearly looking for what can be common to absolutely opposing arguments.

The aim of this flowchart is to elucidate how contradiction works, showing how different arguments are capable of building a chain of questions and new ideas, through what is dissimilar and also what is common in contradictory positions. *Euthydemus* recounts difficult and complex dialogues between sophists and philosophers, how dogs and cats illustrate heated and rich conversations, in which we have all kinds of contradictory arguments that ennoble and clarify the contradiction.

In both Antiphon's and Plato's works, one can see what is described in the flowchart: an overvaluation of the pro arguments, i.e. those that aim to elucidate their positive behavior, such as proving their innocence or even diminishing their guilt, contextualizing ways of benefiting from the conflict. On the other hand, the role of the arguments against is based on a devaluation of any argument that combats what has been defended in the arguments for, in other words, arguments with a contrary connotation that emphasize the negative conduct of the subject of the dispute.

Thinking about the relationship between pros and cons, we can see how the works analyzed are well suited to this study, because throughout their content they clearly present these situations, allowing us to better observe the phenomenon of contradiction. This point, as exemplified by the flowchart, is present in the middle of the so-called "combat", because it illustrates well what happens in the middle of the battlefield, where on both sides we have fighters armed with the power to counter-argue.

CHAPTER I - CONTRADICTION IN DIFFERENT SCENARIOS

1.1. Contradiction in Greece

The *Sophist Movement* is a work that allows us to understand how the changes that took place in Greece are linked to the sophists, together with the role of contradiction in this scenario and its influence in this field. The period lived in Athens in the 5th century BC faces a series of obstacles to its proper understanding, since there are no complete writings left by any of the known sophists, with only fragments and summaries, often obscure and confusing, to be used as research objects. Another problematic factor in the analysis of these thinkers is the fact that the philosopher Plato was one of the greatest suppliers of information about the Sophists, but was also their greatest critic, treating them in an extremely hostile manner. In the dispute between the Sophists and Plato, the latter was considered the right one for a long time, and the Sophists the wrong one. Thus, as G.B. Kerferd says in 2003: "there is a kind of half-life between the pre-Socratics on the one hand, and Plato and Aristotle on the other." In this way, the Sophists always seem to wander like "lost souls"[1] among the philosophers, neither being recognized as great thinkers nor having their abilities properly known. The period from 450 to 400 BC was a remarkable one for the city of Athens, as it underwent countless changes, both social and political, and is known as Athens' greatest epoch, due to the great diversity of events that made it possible to renew Athenian society.

In this context, many standards were harshly attacked and the Sophistic movement was extremely important in expressing all these transformations and the transition from poetic culture to the effective formation of the *polis*. The need to better understand the relativism brought about by Sophistic art was an inherent point in the mutations undergone at that time. It should be emphasized that the history of previous attempts to evaluate the Sophists is essential for a better understanding, together with the historical and social situation that produced the activity of these thinkers.

Plato's hostility towards the Sophists is notorious and has always been recognized by researchers in the field. However, since he was one of the main sources of information about the Sophists, it is necessary to analyze his works. The conclusions made by Plato are not scientific, as they are not based on "rational principles and are incapable of providing explanations"[2] . His research into sophistry is empirical in nature and in most of his works he treats the sophists with a certain antipathy. As a result, this philosopher often defines them as "a paid hunter of rich young men", "a man who sells virtue" or even "a sophist is someone who entertains controversies of the kind called

---

1KERFERD, 2003, p.10, 11 and 12.
2KERFERD, 2003, p. 13.

eristica"[3] , among others.

Faced with this series of unequivocal condemnations, the Sophists built their history on the reputation of not being serious thinkers who had no relevance in the history of philosophy, along with the fact that their knowledge was considered immoral. However, in the first half of the 19th century, this idea was reformulated because, with the development of new approaches to history, it was noticed that the Sophists were being mischaracterized. And their relativism was being exaggerated by the Platonic and Aristotelian reading.

The name sophist comes from the Greek words *sophos* and *sophia*, which mean "wise" and "wisdom". The term *Sophia has* always been associated with a kind of wisdom that was not granted to all mortals, but belonged only to the poet, the seer and the sage. As soon as a sophist was considered a professional in their field, they were entitled to charge a fee, so they were innovators compared to the others of their time.

The fact that the sophists charged fees displeased a number of people, because they claimed that virtue and wisdom were not things to be sold. What bothered them most was the fact that the sophists "sold" their art to men who could afford to pay for their teachings. This was seen by many as something wrong, but if we look at this behavior today, we see an art that is accessible to all, with the aim of instructing those who are interested.

Therefore, the fact that men with money, i.e. those considered wealthy at the time, were able to pay for the teaching offered by the sophists was clearly what displeased the other thinkers. This was because they would lose their "status" of superiority in society and become equal to anyone else. Thus, anyone who could afford the services of the sophists could learn the techniques to become an efficient and successful politician.

The first step taken to reformulate the role of the sophists in philosophy was the concept created by Hegel with regard to the term "dialectic"; it gave rise to a benchmark for the study of Plato and, in a way, enabled a better understanding of the eristics practiced by the sophists in the face of the differences addressed in Plato's dialectic. Hegel saw dialectics as follows:

The movement of his thinking follows the universal pattern for all thought: it begins by formulating a positive thesis which is then denied by the antithesis. Moving on, thought produces a synthesis of thesis and antithesis, and the process continues with the synthesis forming the thesis of a new cycle, each time, until everything that was implicit in the original starting point has become explicit.[4]

Thus, we have the concept of dialectics as something that doesn't accept as true anything that it

3KERFERD, 2003, p. 14.
4 KERFERD, 2003, p. 18.

hasn't itself approved, with an incessant search for something absolute and without edges, in other words, something solid that doesn't allow for doubt, but only with the aim of truth above all.

According to Hegel, Greek philosophy was the result of three periods: the period from Thales to Aristotle, the second, Hellenistic times and the third, the era of Neoplatonism. The period that interests us is the first, because it deals with the Sophists, Socrates and the followers of Socrates. By portraying the Sophists as subjectivists, Hegel manages to reinsert them into the history of philosophy. Thus, through the principle of subjectivity, according to which "it is assumed that it is the thinking and perceiving subject himself who determines his own thoughts and perceptions". [5] thus gave birth to the characterization of the sophists, beings who self-determined their thoughts, free from absolute truths, as the dialecticians preached.

The Sophists were accepted as subjectivists throughout the 19th century and into the first third of the 20th century. However, their reputation took a dark turn, given that "truth and reality were objective, not subjective", so Plato's questions were still being widely accepted[6] . Thus, defending the Sophists' point of view was tantamount to denying the moral values that were so traditional and sacred at the time.

The main purpose of George Grote's work was to re-evaluate the sophists, and in the sixty-seventh chapter of *the History of Greece*, he saw them as "champions of intellectual progress"[7] , and also stated that they were "teachers who simply represented the opinions current in their time"[8] . In defense of the Sophists, Grote claimed that they were not a school or a sect, but a profession with no doctrinal community. With this argument, it was possible to show the others that the questionable conduct of one sophist could not affect the others. Another point discussed was the fact that they taught immoral doctrines, since this question was not supported even by Plato, the main fighter against the sophists.

In view of Grote's analysis, the sophists gained general acceptance, because "it was simply not a historical fact that they had poisoned and demoralized the Athenian moral character by corrupt teaching"[9] , so the fame of the sophists was greatly defended. Another author contributed, Wilhem Nestle[10] , when he wrote that the sophists were now different from the philosophers in terms of the object they dealt with, since the latter studied men in society; dealing with "subjective knowledge for practical purposes, to ensure dominion over men and life, whereas the philosopher deals with knowledge for knowledge's sake".

5KERFERD, 2003, p. 19.
6KERFERD, 2003, p. 19
7KERFERD, 2003, p. 20
8GROTE, 1846, p. 56 *apud* KERFERD.2003, p.20.
9 KERFERD, 2003, p. 21
10Ibid. I.2, 6th ed., 1291-6.

In a positive view of the sophists, there was more concern with what they did and were than with what they thought, so it was an approach in which the sophists were inspired by an educational ideal of rhetoric, seen as masters of the ideal of political virtue, aiming for success in life in all its aspects.

1.2. The Contradiction of the Sophists

Even today it is difficult to define the sophists and their role in Antiquity, but based on the readings that guide this work, it is possible to know their historicity, as the term *sophistés* itself was used in its origin as a synonym for *sophós* which means wise[11] . Thus, the sophists presented themselves as "new masters", those who knew how to speak, with an enviable rhetoric and social and political value; this virtue was due to the highly convincing way in which they communicated, achieving consensus through their own reasoning.

In the work *The Sophists*[12] by Mário Untersteiner, there is a polemical approach to the Sophists that fits in perfectly with our work, questioning the fact of contradiction in the Sophistic world. He writes that "the sophists agree on an anti-idealist concreteness that does not follow the path of skepticism, but rather that of a realism and phenomenism that does not confine reality to a single dogmatic scheme, but allows it to reign with all its contradictions, There is always a conflict that leads to contradiction, allowing a kind of "multiplicity of experience", allowing the birth or death of new conceptions within us, but much of this reasoning is something invisible, that is, it can only be "understood within the general scheme of thought of the philosopher".

Kerferd's work states that the sophists represented an abandonment of physical speculation in the direction of something new. This statement defines well the important role of the sophists in the history of Greece, since they innovated the way of thinking of an entire people by implementing new elements capable of shaping various types of thought.

The sophist had his own way of creating speeches and the technique used to teach others. One method of teaching that was widely used was that of questions and answers associated with the ability to speak briefly, thus being considered speeches surrounded by truths about things[13] .

Through the power of language, the sophists were able to transform things so that they appeared large or small, and even so that new things appeared old and vice versa. Thus, these thinkers discovered both the conciseness of arguments and contradiction through the art of discourse.

A good example of this art can be seen in the work of the sophist Antiphon, whose book *Tetralogies is* an imaginary rivalry, explaining a chain of arguments that are totally contradictory to each other,

11CASSIN, 2005.
12UNTERNSTEINER, 1967 *apud* KERFERD, 2003, p. 25.
13KERFERD, 2003, p. 58.

but which brilliantly echo the way in which this phenomenon emerges that is so important and constitutive for the Greek city: the art of contradiction.

It should be noted that in the next two chapters, Plato's work *Euthydemus* will be the subject of our studies, since it portrays the phenomenon of contradiction in its dialogues with great praise and through the clear clash between these two works, it will be possible to extract a clearer idea of this fascinating but little explored theme.

CHAPTER II - THE CONTRADICTORY GENIUS OF ANTIPHON

Throughout the *Tetralogies we can* see Antiphon's own ability to rival himself, but especially in the *Tetralogies* this characteristic is most clearly demonstrated; the purpose of this study is precisely to diagnose the influence and implicit presence of contradiction in each case proposed, since when he delivers two speeches, one for the prosecution and one for the defense, the author describes them equally brilliantly in the following cases: accusation against the stepmother of murder by poisoning; *Tetralogy* I and II: anonymous murder and *Tetralogy* III: murder trial against what is said to be guiltless. When analyzing the work *Testimonies, Fragments and Speeches of the* Athenian Antiphon, in order to portray and critically approach the different points of view of the author, the ability of the same person to develop two totally contrary theses will be emphasized, demonstrating his ability to defend them with the same genius. This ability expressed by the sophist proves how contradiction is in the structure of an argument and can be the main guide of a discourse that reveals inconsistencies observed in one or other point of view. The aim is thus to compose a single double structure, "capturing" the best of each of the two arguments. There is a lot to observe in the work in question, and the main approach of this study is to find the main contradictions and antitheses that make up the discourses.

2.1. *Testimonies, fragments and speeches*

Antiphon's *Tetralogies* consist of a set of four speeches, beginning with the accuser's speech, followed by the defender's reply and then a second speech from each side. These are schematic models of discourse that enable the reader to extract from their content a clear idea of how the accusation and defense act in the cases narrated by the sophist.

It should be noted that a considerable number of his writings have not survived the passage of time, so some of Antiphon's writings are not complete, but only fragments, and there are cases in his work where only the accusation is present and the defense is lacking.

The speech written by the sophist portrays a multiple Antiphon, and in antiquity the suspicion arose as to whether there was more than one Antiphon, due to their disparate speeches in content and form. Faced with such different perceptions from the same person, the *Tetralogies* emerged, staging two reciprocally opposing speeches about the same thing.

In the case of the accusation against the stepmother, who is accused of murdering her husband by poisoning him, it begins with the son of the deceased making a complaint against the stepmother and, in view of his inexperience, presenting himself to the judges of the time in order to prove the stepmother's guilt through a speech surrounded by emotion and family conflicts.

In *Tetralogy* I, the division of the discourse is different, as the subject is not presented in the introductions, because the author has not fully ascertained the fact. In this *Tetralogy,* the murder of a master and his slave is analyzed, and right from the start there is a complete denial about who committed the murder, followed by the question of premeditated deliberation and, moreover, how the decision was made. In this episode there is evidence of the slave's testimony, followed by a digression and an epilogue.

Tetralogy II deals with the case of two young men who were exercising and one ended up hitting the other while throwing darts, thus beginning a series of questions about the issue of involuntary manslaughter. A discussion begins in which, on the one hand, there is reciprocal incrimination and, on the other, there is a displacement of the issue.

Finally, we have *Tetralogy* III, which deals with a murder involving a young man and a gentleman who die as a result of the fight in which they both fell. In this case, the young man says that he is not to blame, because the gentleman was the one who initiated the blows, which the young man considers to be unjust. From there begins a series of mutual incriminations between the young man and those considered to be "avengers of the dead".

Regarding the *Tetralogies* described by Antiphon, one point stands out in all of them: the involuntariness of the acts. It is important to pay attention to this characteristic, before going into the specific cases, because this way it becomes possible to show how Antiphon aims to demonstrate "two types of criminal conduct, that which involves only the planning of the crime and that which involves direct participation in the crime, through the use that the murderer makes of his own hands to kill the victim"[14] .

Unintentional acts can occur in a number of ways, whether through error or ignorance when performing a particular action or even through negligence, recklessness or

The exclusion of the responsibility of the coercive agent is the basis of most of the speeches narrated by the sophist, since, through the persuasion of discourse, it would be possible to eliminate the authorship of some crime by addressing the issue of the involuntariness of the suspect. Thus, many dialogues do not seek the causes of the crime in the act of the defendant, but rather in the conduct of the victim himself, as a way for the accused to give the accuser the same story, but in a different sphere, in terms of the poles of the action and his culpability.

With this in mind, the argument of the speaker of the *Tetralogies is* full of sentimentality, suffering and pain. And it will be through this discourse that Antiphon will give the air of tragedy to each

---

14 MacDowell, 1989, p.111-116 *apud* SILVA, 2014, p. 276. impericia. Such conduct falls within the field of lack of intentionality, i.e. there is no will to commit a crime. In this way, the person carries out the act without aiming for the end result and without prior anticipation of what is desired, in this case, a premeditated crime.

episode narrated, initiating a complete reversal of roles and perspectives, in which thinking the opposite of what is thought becomes a ghost for the conflicting parties, making it difficult to know who is really responsible for certain criminal conduct.

Thus, what is at stake for Antifonte is not exactly the letter of the law or a particular legal institute, but rather the vision of a "sophisticated theoretical battle that aims to delineate more clearly the nature of criminal responsibility"[15] . However, there is a slight contradiction in the cases described by Antiphon when it comes to demonstrating that a crime is premeditated and, at the same time, involuntary.

Regarding the contradiction in Antiphon's work, it can be seen that the orator doesn't try to prove his innocence, let alone argue whether or not there was premeditation. This is because what he really has to prove and vigorously defend are the mistakes made by his opponents, both in conducting the trial and in raising a "false" accusation.

In view of this, it becomes necessary to go into the cases exposed in the work, as a way of facilitating and synthesizing the ideas and reasons that moved Antiphon to develop such a complex and paradoxical work.

2.1.1. Stepmother charged with murder by poisoning

The speech against the stepmother is the only accusatory speech by Antiphon to which we have access today; this text offers us a contextualization of the universe in which it is set, based on comments about social, political and cultural issues in Athens. It is possible to notice the transposition of various categories of style, which have a remarkable persuasive force and contribute to the construction of the *pathos of* the discourse.

This story portrays the accusation against the stepmother for the murder of her husband by poisoning; it is important to note that the stepmother was a common figure in Athenian society in the 4th and 5th centuries and this character was surrounded by stories of negative characteristics, being seen as a village that either mistreated the stepchildren or the husband himself, so the stepmother already had a stereotypical pattern, by definition, as an evil woman.

The beginning of the story is somewhat confusing, as it interweaves a double murder of two men by their concubines. The first victim is called Filoneo and is a friend of the father of the speaker, i.e. the son who accuses his stepmother. This man had formed a bad opinion of his concubine and threatened to have her committed to a brothel, making her angry. In this scenario, the stepmother and the concubine got along well because, as well as being neighbors, they shared a common feeling: a lack of love for their husbands.

15SILVA, 2014, p. 249

The two women get together and consider the possibility of killing their husbands with poison. From then on, they set the whole thing up during a party while the men were making a common libation and, to end the lives of their companions, they mix poison in their drink. Filoneo dies right there because he had drunk too much, while the speaker's father, because he had drunk less, only contracted a disease.

The accuser, i.e. the victim's son, filed a complaint against the stepmother on the basis that she and her children did not want to hand over the slaves for questioning, and that this attitude was extremely suspicious. The accuser had no concrete evidence as to the perpetrator of the crime and presented himself to the judges in a modest manner, recognizing his young age and inexperience. He made great use of emotional appeals in order to automatically gain the sympathy of the jurors by inciting antipathy for the opposing party through his qualities, such as his modesty and humility.

Although I have no knowledge of the defense presented in the case, there is a good chance that the jurors were convinced and shared a certain fear of the woman and admired the son's loyalty to his father, which was seen as an important issue in Athenian society at the time.

The young man's questions are based on the fact that the dead cannot be left without revenge and, above all, the fact that his father was killed voluntarily and that he was the victim of premeditation, which makes the accuser full of strength to fight his stepmother and her children.

The fact that the stepmother's children supported them and did not agree with the interrogation of the slaves was further proof for the accuser that the stepmother was guilty. In order to arrive at the truth of the facts, the slaves' confirmations were needed, but as soon as they stopped putting the facts to the test, they proved to be guilty. There's no way of knowing what you don't know about or don't want to know, so it wouldn't be possible to know the truth of something you haven't learned.

Thus, it can be seen that Antiphon worked the entire speech on the basis of emotional appeal, starting from the argument that because of the refusal of the half-siblings to interrogate the slaves in order to verify what had happened - the only significant argument in the speech - he begins a vivid narrative, full of metaphors and tragic images that, as well as appealing directly to the emotional side of the jurors, also do so indirectly by making a connection between the stepmother and the mythological stereotype of her husband's murderer - represented by Clytemnestra (a mythological character, wife of Agamemnon, who premeditated his murder in revenge for the sacrifice of her daughter Iphigenia).

The speaker reaffirms at all times that he provided all the possibilities to find out what was behind his father's murder, but, faced with the complete denial of all the procedures he had outlined in relation to his stepmother's children, he became convinced that they were involved in the crime.

The accuser himself states that he "pursued his father's murderer with righteousness and justice", until he came across suspicions involving his own family.

In addition to the aspects relating to the negative characterization of the stepmother, the question of the son's loyalty to his father in contrast to the half-brothers' loyalty to the stepmother is also a strong appeal to the juri. In this speech, the speaker, the victim's son, makes it clear that the case in question is a murder committed by his stepmother with intent and premeditation, and addresses his plea to the judges:

I beseech you, brave judges, if I prove that their mother is the murderer of our father with intent and premeditation, and that not once, but many times, she has been caught red-handed plotting his death, be, first of all, avengers of your laws, which you have received from the gods and your descendants and according to which you judge every time you condemn, and, secondly, be helpers of the dead man and, at the same time, of me who have been left alone.[16]

The question of whether or not he should be questioned is the most contradictory element in this whole episode, highlighting how elements that can often go unnoticed hold a multiplicity of meanings that are often unexplored. Thus, as the speaker himself states, the fact that he opts for this procedure and the accuser dismisses it already shows, from his point of view, evidence against him. The most interesting thing is that the accuser himself says that if the stepmother's children and the stepmother dismissed the slaves for questioning and the speaker didn't accept, these indications would be in favor of the accused, in other words, the speaker himself could be pointed out as a suspect.

At this point, the expertise of the orator, now the author of the work, Antiphon, becomes apparent. Because in order to score points in his favor and influence the verdict of the judges, he doesn't just focus his speech on the issue of breaking the law, or on confirming guilt or innocence by listing a multitude of proofs and witnesses. As a rule, the orators presented by the sophist made their work before the judges become one:

critical judgment of the rhetorical resources that seem to contribute to the establishment of evidence that is composed in view of the choice they make in adopting the serious, grandiose, solemn and tragic stylistic resource that characterizes prayers, supplications and exhortations.[17]

Therefore, it was based on the tenor of each speech that success was sought or not. The best staging based on emotion would define which side would convince the judges. Thus, as researcher Anna Christina da Silva states:

one can read Antiphon's speeches by comparing them with Clytemnestra's speeches, considering them as a

16ANTIFONTE, 2008, p. 119.
17 SILVA, 2014, p. 122/123.

collection of verbal artifices that reveal the orator's accentuated taste for the themes of the tricks of lachrymose chatter and the dangerous deception of the lament that always evokes an unfortunate fate.[18]

Since the evidence is scarce, only a relevant argument can convince the jury of the stepmother's guilt. For this reason, it is important to value, in the translation, these stylistic aspects that make this a bold and strong work and show between the lines characteristics that, after careful analysis, make a big difference in the construction of the discourse.

The way in which the stepmother's conduct is presented as intentional or not is a point worth highlighting, as it is directly related to whether or not it is an involuntary act, as described at the beginning of this chapter. What we see is a fusion between the stepmother's intentionality and the rhetoric present in the speeches, in other words, whether or not something is contested is what enables those involved in a case to use their words to create what is most beneficial to them.

In this way, we are faced with the possibility of reinventing ourselves all the time through the contradictions of discourse, "dialogical freedom and the despotic use of words"[19] which are the key to this innovative experience that will allow us to extract from rhetoric all that is most valuable in it. In this sense, we have the greatness of contradiction and the way in which it opens up new ideas and concepts.

2.1.2. *Tetralogy* I: Anonymous Murder Case

This discourse deals with an event that took place between a couple made up of a master and a slave who returned from a dinner party and were found freshly stabbed to death; after their deaths, a relative of the master who was killed accused an enemy of his as having committed the murder, but the other denied it. This leads to a dispute about the personalities of those involved.

The discourse of accusation vigorously defends the guilt of the enemy of the Lord killed by blows, because, in addition to the fear of accusing an innocent person, leaving the real culprit unpunished and consequently staining the honor of the city, as preached by ancient customs; we were facing an alleged murderer who was explicitly a declared enemy of the deceased Lord, leaving no doubt for the accusers of his responsibility in the crime.

The prosecution ruled out any other possibility of death, such as an accident or robbery, because, apart from the blows suffered by both victims, nothing was stolen from them, as the following statement shows:

It's unrealistic that the crime was committed by bandits: no one in extreme danger of their life would let a profit that was at their disposal go to waste, as the victims were found wearing their clothes. Nor did anyone

18SILVA, 2014, p. 128.
19SILVA, 2014, p. 128.

kill him because he was drunk, as he would have been recognized by his drinking companions. Nor was it because of a dispute, as they wouldn't be fighting at that time of night in a deserted place. Nor would he have wanted to hit someone else, because he wouldn't have killed them along with the slave. Having ruled out any other hypothesis of suspension, the death itself points to him as having killed by premeditated deliberation.[20]

The "absolute certainty" of the accusation consists of the fact that the defendant is a long-time enemy of the victim, given that the accuser has already instituted several lawsuits against the accused and has not been victorious in any of them. Recently the defendant was being sued by the victim, "under the deposit of two talents, for theft of sacred wealth"[21] . Following the above, the prosecution believes that it is probable that the accused deliberated in a premeditated way in order to repel the blows that he might suffer as a result of the existence of these lawsuits; the prosecution further states that:

The desire for revenge seized him and made him forget the dangers; the fear of circumstantial evils, which stunned him, made him hotter and led him to get down to work. He hoped that with these actions, he would be covered up as a murderer and even escape the accusation <of theft>, because no one would turn against him and the cause would be abandoned. [22]

Verisimilitude is an important concept dealt with by Antiphon who demonstrates, through this consideration, how the veracity of facts is achieved, especially in the description of the *Tetralogies*. When we look at this trait from the point of view of the sophist, we see the search for a concept that demonstrates a "supposed appearance of truthfulness as opposed to the reality of truth"[23] . In this context, given the lack of written laws, there is a certain orientation through verisimilitude that allows the judges involved to understand through the narration of the facts how the crime was committed.

The chain and the play of verisimilitude are the guiding ideas that govern the accuser, there is a kind of confrontation between appearance and reality[24] that allows judges to draw an idea from within a set of arguments, that is, from a whole you can draw a bigger idea that reflects in the judges a thought that did not previously exist.

In this way, the concept dealt with here enables an explanation with a wealth of detail, leading judges to the "domain of the evidence of a demonstration"[25] . Everything that can be said can be produced through speeches, narratives, arguments and objections; the birth of verisimilar elements that surround each other, forming or at least trying to contemplate what we call the truth of the

---

20ANTIFONTE, 2008, p.131.
21 ANTIFONTE, 2008, p.133.
22ANTIFONTE, 2008, p.133.
23 SILVA, 2014, p.114.
24SILVA, 2014, p.114.
25 SILVA, 2014, p.115.

facts.

Based on the concept of verisimilitude proposed by Antiphon, it can be seen in this *Tetralogy* that when the case is presented to the judges, the murder will be exposed as intentional and premeditated; since, by analyzing the same circumstances from a new perspective, it is possible to create a new assessment of the same facts, thus changing the focus of suspicions when the verisimilitudes are confronted.

There is a clash between contradiction and verisimilitude, as if on the one hand there is the contradiction that arises in the singularity of the radically different opinions of the interlocutors and on the other, there is the emergence of a new understanding of the crime, through dramatic representations and speeches interpreted by the speaker. As if it were possible to think of a contradiction in common and truthful elements.

The defendant, in addition to exercising his defense in order to get rid of the charges, would have to prove who the murderers really were. The contradiction in this case lies in the fact that the defendant was a recognized enemy of the victim, which would make him the main suspect and this would be a stupid act, since such an attitude would give him away as the main suspect.

In this *Tetralogy*, it can be seen that the defense's main argument is the clear image of a great contradiction, given that the fact that those involved in a crime are long-time enemies, recognized by everyone in society, is the main point used by the accused, because, since they are both declared enemies, the enmity that surrounds them is used as proof that he didn't kill him because he knew that the blame would fall entirely on him, finally, it can be seen that the basic argument of the prosecution and the defense are based on the same thesis: the enmity between the two and have the same content. However, their interpretations are totally contrary and different.

2.1.3. *Tetralogy* II: Involuntary Manslaughter Trial

The subject of the speech is an episode involving two teenagers who were practicing throwing darts in a gymnasium. After one of the youngsters threw his projectile according to the rules of the sport, he injured the other who was exercising while running around the gym and ran into the path of the spear, causing the latter's death. As the story goes, the father accuses the thrower of murder, who shifts the blame for the blow onto the runner.

The prosecution and the defense are represented by the parents of the teenagers involved. The prosecution begins its argument by saying that this was an unfortunate accident, but that it was duly witnessed and characterized. This observation could be the culmination of the problem to be discussed:

The facts on which there is agreement have been judged by the law or the decrees, which are the masters of every republic. If, however, there is any dispute, it is up to you, citizen men, to decide. In fact, I don't think the accused will have anything to contest against me, because my son, struck in the back in a gymnasium by this young man's spear, died instantly. I don't accuse him of having killed voluntarily, but involuntarily (...) I ask you to have pity on the parents deprived of their son, to deplore the premature death of the victim, to expel him from all the places from which the law expels the murderer, and not to tolerate the whole city being stained because of him.[26]

Thus, the victim's father presents positive elements that confirm the truth of the facts, using the evidence of everything that happened without worrying about explaining a strongly persuasive speech, unlike the way his adversary uses in his defense speeches.

When defending his son, the defendant's father doesn't aim to create any superficial points about the facts, but only to use the discourse narrated by the prosecution and remove its argumentative flaws. The defense does not build a discourse that attacks the externalization of the facts, but rather confronts a single view of them, that is, the defense discourse will work with the idea of diversity of unity that guarantees a different interpretation of the same concrete fact. This method is the synthesis of contradiction.

The first part of the prosecution's speech is based on the question of the unintentionality of the thrower, but the fact that it was unintentional does not diminish the father's intentions for a just punishment and the unhappiness of being deprived of his son. The second phase of the accusation forces the father to acknowledge that the defense had an advantage in his speech considering the resources used, but he claims to have done nothing, as the following excerpt describes:

I, who have done nothing wrong, suffering miserable and terrible punishments, and now even more terrible, by action and not by word, seek refuge in you and pray for your mercy. O men, avengers of impious actions, connoisseurs of the pious, do not let yourselves be persuaded by the perverse subtlety of speeches, contrary to the evidence of actions, and do not falsely conceive the truth of facts.[27]

The classification of the crime is another point worth highlighting, since there is an inversion of the responsibility of those involved outlined in the defense's speech, defining that the causes of death should not be sought in the actions of the defendant, but in the actions of the victim. At this point, there is a direct confrontation in the accusations of involuntary crime addressed by the prosecution, demonstrating that responsibility for the crime will be the biggest problem in this case.

The reasons behind the father mourning his son's untimely death are strengthened by the suspicion that the wrongs his son has suffered will not be avenged:

The law proclaims that murderers should be punished, because the one who kills involuntarily is right to fall

26ANTIFONTE, 2008, p. 151
27ANTIFONTE, 2008, p. 158 and 159.

into involuntary harm, and the one who perishes is no less harmed if it is involuntary rather than voluntary, and it would be unjust for him to be left without revenge[28] .

Voluntary and involuntary acts once again gain ground in Antiphon's texts, demonstrating how this question of intentionality or not causes clashes in the disputes in question. More precisely, the involuntary crime does not condemn the accused, and it is relevant at this point what actually led the victim to act negligently and consequently cause his own death.

The first speech in the defense of the young man who threw the dart works with the idea that the fatality that befell the young man was caused by "the dead man himself", so that because of his mistaken and reckless conduct he "wronged himself", as the father says in his son's defense:

If the javelin had been moving outside the determined limits when it hit the boy in front of it, there would have been no discourse that would have freed us from having committed murder. But the boy was running under the trajectory of the dart, to which he placed his body, preventing the other from eventually reaching the target and receiving the blow of the spear towards which it was directed, so we are not to blame. [29]

The second defense speech consolidates the importance of the structuring arguments of the discourse, defending the need for plausible justifications before someone can be blamed for a death. In defending himself against the accusations, the pitcher's father blames the victim himself and is convinced of his son's innocence:

My son, having committed no wrongdoing, would not be right to be punished on behalf of the one who did wrong, since it is enough for him to bear his own mistakes; the other boy, however, did wrong at the same time and was punished for it. Once the murderer has been punished, the murder will not go unpunished.[30]

But then there is the final accusatory speech, which concerns the speaker's indignation at the audacious and infamous arguments put forward by the accused.

That necessity forces everyone to speak and act against nature, this man seems to me to show, not by word, but by deed. Until now, he was the least impudent and the least daring of men; today, constrained by his own misfortune, he speaks in a way I never thought he could. For my part, taken by great folly, I didn't suspect that he would contradict[31] .

At this point, we can see that the ability to produce contradiction is at stake, and it will be from this challenge that a "winner" will emerge. Antiphon proposes, through this moment of discourse, to demonstrate the direct confrontation of two opposing rhetorics. Understanding the philosophical nature of the *Tetralogies* is a difficult task, but when analyzed from the perspective of the operations carried out in the Courts, the role of both the contradiction and the impact that

---

28ANTIFONTE, 2008, p.160.
29 ANTIFONTE, 2008, p.155.
30 ANTIFONTE, 2008, p.165.
31 ANTIFONTE, 2008, p.157.

Antiphon's arguments have on readers becomes more evident.

This *Tetralogy* brings an inversion in the poles of the process regarding the question of who is the real culprit in the death; the defense supports the thesis that the culprit is the victim himself, because the mistake was made by the young man who ran towards the wrong place and caused his own misfortune. In this way, the defense understands that the mistake of this young man absolves the accused; there is a great contradiction because there was in fact a victim, whoever is found guilty, the defense was extremely bold in making a speech in which it defends itself and at the same time accuses, creating a transposition in the whole process. The ability of contradiction to find its greatest ally in the most controversial points has therefore been demonstrated, i.e. death itself is the content of contradictory interpretations of what happened, whether it be the guilt of the shooter or the boy who died.

2.1.4. *Tetralogy* III: Murder trial against what is said to be guiltless

Tetralogy III illustrates the murder case against a young man who claims to be blameless, that is, he claims not to be responsible for the criminal conduct, since he was only defending himself, thus claiming self-defense. The events took place between an elderly man and a young man who, as a result of an injury, got into a fight, because the young man struck harder and was physically fitter than the man, and the latter died as a result. Because of this, someone accuses the young man of having committed murder, starting a series of mutual accusations in which, on the one hand, we have the young man defending himself by claiming that he had only defended himself against the man's blows and, on the other, we have the accusation of the fact that the victim was elderly and that such an episode was a total lack of respect for the values and customs of the time.

In the case in question, the victim seems to be a senile man who, overcome by the excesses of alcoholic beverages, assaults for no apparent reason a young man who has more strength and audacity to return the blows he has suffered. Thus, the personal characteristics of those involved are used in a striking way in each of the speeches and allow us to better understand the moral and legal concepts belonging to this *Tetralogy*.

The accusation explores the value of human life, emphasizing the need to avoid death before the consummation of old age, defending what is considered morally good and which values should be respected. In this way, it becomes essential to punish young people who have violated the social prescriptions that order them not to commit any wrong against the elderly. The relevance of human existence is directly linked to respect for and obedience to the gods, as is demonstrated in the following passage: "since our lives have been deemed worthy of value by the God, he who kills another unlawfully commits impiety towards the gods, as well as circumventing the legal prescriptions of men."[32] .

The accuser is astonished by the opposite discourse, claiming that regardless of who started the unjust blows, the one who strikes back to the point of causing his opponent's death should be held responsible for that action. At this point, if we look at the verisimilar facts, we can see that through judicial rhetoric the young man aims to present the judges with a form of counter-argument that determines elements that indicate how the victim's own conduct was a determining factor in his death. But it was not only the character of the dead man that determined his tragic end. It's time to show the judges that the old man, although seriously wounded, survived the blows and died after being entrusted to the care of a less than competent doctor.

Thus, there is a transposition, in which the accused transfers the responsibility for the victim's murder to the doctor who took care of her, and the defense therefore becomes an accusation in retaliation. The young man claims that the blows were unjustly inflicted by the elderly man who was drunk, and that the latter is to blame for his own misfortune, since the young man only repelled the attacks he suffered and did not consider his self-defense actions to be unjust. The accused's basic argument refers to the fact that the victim did not die at the same time as he received the blows. That said, the young man does not consider that the elderly man was killed by him, blaming this on an incompetent doctor and not as a result of his blows. The accused claims that other doctors warned the doctor in question that if the patient was treated with the therapy he used, he would risk dying, which in fact happened. With regard to the doctor's incompetence - an argument put forward by the prosecution - the defense sees it as a failure due to inexperience, ruling out the possibility of the doctor's guilt.

At this point, we return to the question of whether or not the doctor's conduct was intentional, as we questioned earlier. Here, there is a confrontation between the conduct of the gentleman, now the victim, the blows dealt by the young man and the conduct of the doctor. All that remains between these characters is the question of who is really responsible for the death and whether or not it was done intentionally.

After a more detailed explanation of the cases and speeches elaborated by Antiphon, it can be seen that contradiction is the basis of the entire structure of his speeches, since it is through the strong points inserted in the arguments of the opposing parties, that there is the starting point for the emergence of the main idea that will curtail the opposing discourse, in other words, when arguing against a certain issue it is as if we were coming up with the opponent's main argument, because it will be through what we defend that the opposing party will base itself to create its main argument.

32ANTIFONTE, 2008, p.167.

By drawing a parallel between *Tetralogies* II and III, it can be seen that they contradict each other on the issue of involuntariness; the first vigorously condemns that the mere fact that the accused's act was involuntary in no way changes or modifies the annoyance and suffering experienced, therefore, whether it was a voluntary act or not, the defendant must be punished fairly and without even contesting these circumstances. On the other hand, in *Tetralogy* III, described above, the prosecution states that in view of the facts, if the young man had killed the elderly man involuntarily, the accused "would deserve some excuse"[33] , which shows how the question of involuntariness can be used in two ways and interpreted in different ways.

2.2. Partial Conclusion: The Ability to Contradict Yourself

The ability to contradict will be the point dealt with now, and it's important to understand what it means to contradict oneself, so let's start with this aspect. When a person is able, when faced with the same fact involving the same people, in the same place with identical characteristics, to take all this information and use it either to affirm a certain point of view or to criticize it, they are capable of contradicting themselves. This was common in the teaching of Greek rhetoric, where young people were given exercises in which they had to raise a thesis and contradict themselves at the same time. This later became known as the equipollence of speeches. There is, however, a fundamental element in this art: all the arguments raised must be coherent and plausible, so that, whether accusing or defending something, it is difficult to take a stand due to the high-level persuasiveness of their speeches. The two arguments about the same content are equally strong, as we saw in the cases cited above.

The art of discourse was inherent to the Greeks, who are generally known for their speeches in the public square and for their rhetoric, which gained prominence in many different areas with the birth of the Greek city and court. As far as the art of speech is concerned, it is undeniable that the sophists were great thinkers capable of persuading crowds with powerful speeches and capable of changing people's minds.

In order to better demonstrate this, we look at Antiphon's work; he gives speeches described by himself in both his accusation and defense, in both of which he structures convincing and logical arguments, allowing the interlocutor to think that they are two authors, and to be surprised by the fact that the same person created concepts and ideas and then confronted them. Such an act is done for the simple pleasure of contradicting oneself.

When you propose an argument and then contradict it, you have an inversion of what used to be considered right and wrong. It's as if there were a key that could be turned two ways in our head,

33 ANTIFONTE, 2008, p.169.

one corresponding to the defense and the other corresponding to the accusation, with the speakers only having to press the one that correlates to our claim.

This way of acting enriches us as thinking beings, because it makes it possible to "break" the chain of pre-established ideas all the time, making new thoughts resurface all the time and also allowing us to understand what is in common between opposing arguments. And it is through this rotation that we will be able to update ourselves, not getting stuck in fixed ideas that limit us as a person.

From now on, we will evaluate how Plato criticized two Sophist brothers who played a continuous game with their speeches and assess whether this game of the brothers can be compared to what Antiphon proposes in a serious way.

CHAPTER III - OTHER WAYS OF CONTRADICTING AND EDUCATING

This chapter will analyze the method used by the sophists in defending their arguments, together with the criticisms pointed out by the anti-sophists from the perspective of Plato's classic work called *Euthydemus*. The aim is to observe how contradiction acts in the sophists' counter-argument procedure and how this art is seen by the thinkers of the time who were also trying to contradict in their own way. It should be noted that the most prominent theme of the *Euthymedeus* is precisely the criticism that Plato makes of the type of verbal dispute practiced by the sophists, known as eristics, which, according to Plato's view, has the sole purpose of winning the dispute at any price. From the anti-sophistic viewpoint, a range of questions opens up about this way of acting and the clear difference between eristics and dialectics.[34]

The book *Euthydemus* takes place in the gymnasium of the Lyceum, where the conversations narrated by Socrates to Criton take place. In addition to these, the following are characters in Euthymedeus: Criton, who was a friend of Socrates; Clinias, the son of Axiochus; Ctesippus, cousin of Menexenus; and the Sophist brothers called Euthymedeus and Dionysodorus. Key players in history, these brothers are seen as the interlocutors of the dialogue, considered to be fighters of words and capable of constructing sophisms; in philosophy, sophism is seen as the act of making specious reasoning, so in a fallacy there would be apparently logical arguments, but which in reality are erroneous and non-conclusive, leading someone to make a mistake within the dialogue. This method was aimed at winning all the battles the sophists waged.

3.1. The game, the fight and the speech

When Euthydemus and Dionysodorus arrive in Athens, Criton shows an interest in meeting them, because when he talks to Socrates, he claims that they are "two very versatile fighters"[35] . But the philosopher assures them that they were not only capable of fighting with their bodies, because they were very skilled in the art of persuasion. Socrates rigorously defended his brothers, saying:

these two are certainly experts in everything [...] for they are expert in fighting with weapons, and are able to make others wise, provided they pay them a salary; then, when it comes to court disputes, they are excellent both at sustaining litigation and at teaching others to speak and to write speeches that are suitable for the courts[36] .

With the arrival of the Sophist brothers and the repercussions of their fame as valuable scholars,

34 KERFERD, 2003, p.18.
35 *Euthydemus,* 271a.
36 *Eutidemo,* 272 d/b.

Socrates showed an interest in learning about the method they practiced, Eristics, in order to become wise and capable of practicing this art. Criton then asks Socrates to explain more about the "knowledge of these men", so that he knows what he is going to learn. At this point, Socrates begins to narrate the conversations in which he, Clinias, Ctesippus, Euthydemus and Dionysodorus take part; the narrator tells us that he was sitting alone in the dressing room when the two Sophist brothers and some of their disciples came in, followed by Clinias and Ctesippus. After greeting them, he said that they were "surely wise men", because they had knowledge of army tactics and commands, but "they are also capable of making him able to assist himself in court if someone commits an injustice against him"[37] .

The brothers disagreed with Socrates and said that their "occupation" was something else, so they both said that they cared for and taught about virtue, because that was what they believed "they were capable of transmitting better and more quickly than any other man"[38] . Faced with this statement, Socrates was overwhelmed and wanted to know if there was any demonstration of what they were defending. At this point, the brothers said that they would demonstrate and were willing to teach their art if anyone was willing to learn.

Thus, a series of questions in order to prove this practice begins, with the aim of demonstrating that the brothers are the best "at exhorting philosophy and the cultivation of virtue"[39] , as Socrates supports. Undaunted, the philosopher proposes that the Sophist brothers teach their wisdom to the young Clinias, so that he can become a wise and virtuous citizen. Fearing that other people will approach the young man, diverting his thoughts down an unworthy path and perverting him, Socrates suggests that Euthydemus and Dionysodorus carry out an experiment on the boy in order to persuade him so that Clinias will see that it is necessary to love wisdom and cultivate virtue.

Faced with this scenario, an attempt is made to demonstrate eristics through the "battle" between Euthydemus and Dionysodorus *versus* Clinias; the questions of knowledge and learning, treated in eristic fashion, deal with arguments based on homonymy, which is when words have the same meaning or pronunciation, but have different meanings. Thus, Euthydemus began by asking Clinias the following question: "Who among men are the *manthânontes* [those who learn/those who understand]: the *sophoi [those* who *know/the* intelligent] or the *amatheis [those who are ignorant/the* stupid]?"[40] . At this point, Dionysodorus, leaning a little closer to Socrates' ear and with a broad smile, said: "I tell you that whichever of the two ways the boy answers, he will be refuted". Faced with Clinias' reply that the intelligent [*sophoi*] are those who learn, Euthydeus said:

37 *Euthydemus,* 273c.
38 *Euthydemus,* 273e.
39 *Eutidemo,* 275.
40 *Eutidemo,* 275d.

29

Some people you call masters, or not? He agreed. And masters are the masters of those who are learning [*manthânontes*], just as the sitarist and the writing master were certainly masters of you and the other children, and you, apprentices, weren't you? - He agreed. - So, while you were learning, you still didn't know the things you were learning, did you? - No, he said - So you were people who knew (*sophoi*) when you didn't know these things? - Of course not, he said. - Therefore, if you are not people who know [*sophoi*], you are ignorant [*amatheis*]   .

Perfectly. - When you learned what you didn't know, it was by being ignorant (*amatheis*) that you learned. - The boy nodded. - It is therefore the *amatheis* [ignorant] who *manthânousin* [learn], and not the *sophoi*, as you believe[41] .

From then on, it was clear, any question that was raised would be easily overturned by the knowledge of the sophists who, as Dioniosidorus himself said: "All questions, Socrates," he said, "we ask like these: no escape."[42] . In this way, the homonymy mentioned above occurs, in a somewhat indirect way, with regard to the meaning of the words "*manthànein*" (learn/understand) and "*suniénai*", because the moment this word is applied to both men who know and those who don't know, or those who know and those who don't know, we have the same word with a double meaning. This was seen by Socrates as a teaching joke, but it was really about eristics and the power of sophistry.

The method used by the Sophist brothers for the so-called enthronement of Clinias, that is, the way they introduce or even launch Clinias into society as a virtuous man, is somewhat ruthless. Through playful and somewhat humiliating put-downs, the Sophist brothers put Clinias in vexatious situations through their word games, creating inner confusion in the young man with the aim of seeing him fall into error or even give up the "battle".

At this point, Socrates, realizing that the brothers were trying to "bring down" the young Clinias by frightening him with their complex arguments, felt obliged to raise the flag of truce to prevent the young man from becoming even more frightened. So, in order to encourage Clinias, Socrates says:

Clinias, don't be surprised if these arguments seem unusual to you.

Perhaps you don't realize the kind of thing the foreigners around you are doing. They're doing exactly what those who take part in the initiation do [...] there's a choir and joking, <as you know,> if you've already been initiated. Now too, these two do nothing but lead a choir around you, and as if dancing, playing, in order to initiate you afterwards. [43]

In line with this thought, it is possible to see that the argumentative magic outlined by the Sophist brothers was surrounded by mockery and games that led nowhere except to the embarrassment of

41 *Euthydemus,* 276b.
42 *Euthydemus,* 276e.
43 *Eutidemo,* 277d.

those who sought such knowledge. In this way, Socrates, realizing that the Sophist brothers have moved away from the true talent that exalted famous Sophists, who used the art of argument correctly, sees himself entitled to demand that the Sophists, after their jokes, demonstrate their "proleptic knowledge" in a serious way[44] .

Therefore, at this point there is a direct confrontation between the correct and erroneous way of using eristics. In view of this, it is necessary to reflect on the generalization of the sophists who have often had their names tarnished in the history of philosophy, due to practitioners such as the brothers Euthydemus and Dionysodorus who, in perfecting the art of eristics, misused it. It is important to note that the misuse of eristics practiced by the brothers is an exception, since the sophists who practiced this art seriously created sublime rhetorical resources, contributing greatly to the conflicts that occurred in the Courts, without the need to "play" as the sophist brothers did.

Finally, the seriousness of the sophists who truly appreciate the art of persuasion and its correct application is essential. They are the ones who, unlike their brothers Euthymedeus and Dionysodorus, adopt this grand, solemn and tragic art[45] capable of winning over crowds with their beautiful speeches surrounded by supplications, prayers and exhortations, and not forgetting the fascination of counter-arguments practiced in a serious and effective way that gives rise to extraordinary contradictions and fallacies.

3.2. The good use of speeches: Socratic counter-argument

The Socratic *epideixis*, i.e. Socrates' exhibition, begins when he wants to demonstrate the relationship between knowledge and virtue, as he himself calls it "in Socratic fashion"[46] , but he does so with a certain fear that he could be "censured" at any moment by the Sophists. In this first interrogation between Clinias and Socrates, the starting point concerns men who desire *eudaimonia*, which is nothing more than happiness itself, linked to the question of living well and being just, in Plato's view. So Socrates begins his explanation of ideas in order to show Clinias the path to wisdom and virtue. It is important to note that Clinias was seen as an apprentice in order to become a fit and virtuous citizen in the society of the time. Raising the banner that all men want to be successful and with the agreement of the young Clinias, his explanation goes in the direction that being successful is not just about being rich, beautiful, healthy, or other qualities concerning the body; good fortune is necessary.

Thus, the fact of having property is reformulated by the arguments raised by Socrates, who reduces good fortune to wisdom. It should be noted that at this point, Socrates raises an important question,

44*Eutidemo,* 278d.
45SILVA, 2014,
46 *Eutidemo,* 278d.

in order to overthrow eristica, by saying that he and the son of Axiochus were talking about the same thing, that is, they had the same concept of goods.

Plato is convinced that the wordplay preached by the Sophists could not triumph if the words that make up a dialogue were properly qualified, i.e. from the moment that the meaning of the words expressed in a discourse has the same meaning for both sides of the conversation, there is a consensus in what is said, enabling clear and equal communication. In this way, it becomes essential that the participants in a dialog work together in search of a common understanding, guaranteeing meanings free of contradiction.

So, from the moment a conversation starts, the words used in that dialogue must have the same meaning. A good example of this can be the way the word "mango" is used: it can be used to refer to fruit or to a piece of clothing. In this way, what Plato defends is the importance of the same word in a conversation having the same meaning for both sides.

Therefore, in the face of contradictory speeches, one way out found by Plato was the fact that in a dialogue the words should have the same meaning for both participants in the dialogue; thus, unlike the sophists who often use ambiguous methods to create confusion in the minds of their opponents, we have from Plato's point of view a way of cutting out this resource used by the sophists.

Socrates takes the floor again and continues his presentation in the *Euthyme*. He concludes that wisdom is good fortune, listing a series of specific professions in which good sense and cunning were necessary for their successful realization, since they would be practiced correctly and the result would be satisfactory. Therefore, if wisdom is present in a certain person, they are fortunate. Socrates complements his thoughts by saying that all goods, whatever they may be, will be reduced to the most precious good, which is wisdom, but it is necessary to profit from this good. Thus, "he who wishes to be happy must not only possess such goods, but must also use them, without which no good comes from their possession"[47] .

In this passage, we can see the importance given to wisdom by Socrates and his friends, demonstrating how they were interested in learning more from the sophists, because they wanted to have their help in order to be able to develop speeches with more eloquence or even strength. At this point, we see a clash between two totally different theories, because, as much as the wisdom of the Sophists was loved by the young people, the philosophers had totally different premises from those preached by the Sophists.

In this way, Socrates tries to show that it is not enough to make men rich, but poor in wisdom, because the way in which goods are treated and used is more important than possessing them. So he

47 *Eutidemo,*280e.

tries to teach the young Clinias, his apprentice, how wise he needs to be in order to manage the benefits provided by the good use of goods.

Thus, Socrates gives a new meaning to a previously limited view in which it was not possible to observe that in the face of the totality of things, what should be taken into account is not the nature of these things in and of themselves, but the way in which they are guided. In other words, if you possess a good and direct it with ignorance, you will cause greater harm than if you didn't possess that good, so if you use your goods with intelligence and wisdom, they will become the greatest goods you can possess[48].

Therefore, by treating a good with attention, it is possible to have lessons and values that not only enhance your assets, but also your essence as a being. We can see that the premises defended by Socrates have a meaning in every action, not just something empty and aimless; we seek meaning in what we do, and that is the truth. Thus, the difference between the playful brothers and the Platonic ones becomes increasingly apparent, because the Sophist brothers act differently, because they don't value seeking a specific meaning for a given thing.

Given this, since all men yearn for happiness, we can see that the desire for this achievement becomes closer the moment we use "things" in the right way, in order to ultimately become the wisest possible, because wisdom is something that is taught not by chance.

The story continues and Socrates gives the floor back to the Sophists, leading to the second erotic confrontation in which Euthydemus and Dionysodorus dispute with Socrates and Ctesippus; in the first round, the Sophistic argument about the impossibility of change is launched and this moment begins with a question from Socrates with the aim of teaching Clinias to be good and wise. Socrates says:

demonstrate to the child what follows: whether he needs to acquire all the sciences, or whether there is only one that he needs to achieve in order to be happy and a good man, and what it is. As I said at the beginning, it is very important for this young man to become wise and good[49].

Then the eldest of the brothers, Dionysodorus, began his speech: "Tell me, Socrates and the rest of you," he said, "all of you who say that you want this young man to become wise: are you joking when you say this, or do you really want it and take it seriously?"[50]. Having asked this question, the sophist continued:

You say you want him to become wise? - Perfectly. - But now, he said, is Clinias wise or not? - Certainly not yet, he says, at least; but he's not one to boast, I said. - But do you, he said, want him to become wise and not

48 *Euthydemus*, 281e.
49 *Eutidemo*, 282e.
50 *Eutidemo*, 282e.

ignorant? - We agreed. - Whoever is not, you want him to become, and whoever is now, to be no more. - When I heard that, I shuddered. While I was still trembling, he said, taking the floor again: "Then, since you want the one who is now to be no more, do you want anything else, it seems, but for him to perish? And really, such friends and lovers would be of great value, to whom it is above all important to annihilate their favorite! [51]

Faced with this speech, tempers flared and once again the Sophists' malice and audacity in the art of counter-arguing became apparent, for Socrates' good intention of starting Clinias on the path of virtue and wisdom was abruptly reversed into another understanding by Dionysodorus. The contradiction was clear at this point, because the same act was interpreted in totally different ways, one with a positive character and the other not. Thus, it is clear to see how the sophists' play on words led the opposite side of the conversation to contradict themselves and make a "mistake", and at that moment the magic of contradiction took place, giving the victory in the round to the sophists.

In the second round, the sophistical argument about the impossibility of what is false arises, so Euthymedeus and Ctesippus have a collision about the things that truly are and the things that are said to be. Thus, the dialogue portrays how it is possible to say or not say what is false, so that one says "things that are in a certain way, but not as they are"[52] . In other words, when you say something, it may have a false character, but if you really say things as they are, you are telling the truth, even if your content contains things that are not.

At this point, there is a clear clash between eristics and dialectics, the confrontation between what truly is and what is said to be true, in other words, the encounter between univocality and relativism, the direct collision between arguments that seek truth based on essence and arguments that recreate themselves in the most varied ways, through what is said, often using the false, in order to win an argument. It's like a fight seen from the outside, where everyone equips themselves with their best weapons and goes into combat, on one side we have the fighters who are looking for an end to give meaning to that fight, who don't want to duel in vain and for whom a greater ideal than just victory would be necessary; on the other hand, on the other side of the ring we have bloodthirsty fighters who take down anyone in front of them with their wordplay and unimaginable skills, warriors who grow with every applause and show of attention, these are courageous and articulate. The former portray the disciples of Plato and the latter the tireless sophists who would know how to defend themselves in court.

As history progresses, the confusion among thinkers increases even more. Faced with this, the sophists try to "clarify" what it means to say things as they are. Ctesippus immediately asks

---

51*Eutidemo,* 283d.
52*Euthydemus,* 284b.

Dionysodorus if there are people who say things as they are, and is promptly answered "[...] there are, of course," he says, "the noble and good, and those who tell the truth [...]"[53] . And Socrates, as a good intermediary, emphasized the qualities of his brothers and asked them to demonstrate their art, but specifically contradiction, because he was immensely interested, along with Ctesippus.

Socrates did this on numerous occasions. Immediately after the brothers' refutations, Socrates would summarize what had happened in the dialogue and then intervene in the events himself, trying to counter-argue and criticize the brothers. The extent and consequences of the argument of the impossibility of the false are the point now dealt with by the philosopher, having been originated by a tense clash between the brothers and Ctesippus. The essential issue concerns the argument put forward by the brothers that Ctesippus intended to annihilate Clinias, when by a development of the argument of being or becoming wise, Dionysodorus says, as mentioned above, that: "Whoever is not, you want him to become, and whoever is now, let him no longer be. [...] So, since you want the one who is now to be no more, do you want anything else, it seems, but for him to perish?"[54] .

Ctesippus is extremely angry at having been accused of wishing Clinias' annihilation, entangled by Dionysodorus' arguments that Clinias' friends wished him not to be what he was. It is in this context that they return to the discussion about the possibility of the false, of error and of contradiction itself, which means mistakenly saying of something that it is, that it isn't, and of something that it isn't, that it is. For example, to say of a computer that it is not a computer is to say something false, as is to say of a pencil that it is a pen. It should be noted that the Sophists wanted to refute the possibility of saying something false, and they play on this when they say that Clinias' friends, in arguing that he should no longer be ignorant, would like to annihilate him, focusing only on non-being as non-existence. Dionisodorus begins his discourse on contradiction by trying to avoid arguments that would lead him into error. In this sense, the question of mistaken attribution would not be on the horizon of the Sophist brothers, who would be defending the impossibility of error so as not to be prevented from using contradictory meanings of certain things at will.

In view of this passage, it can be seen that the Sophists viewed contradiction in a totally different way to Plato's disciples, since for them the starting point for contradictory dialogues was the fact that in the same conversation the statements and words had different meanings, in other words, the words used in a discussion should be properly qualified, having a univocal character in their content and way of understanding so that they had the same meaning for all the participants in the conversation. Thus, statements should be about each thing as it is, with a direct link to the question

53 *Eutidemo,* 284d.
54 *Euthydemus,* 283c/283d

of essence.

At this point, the question arises as to when contradiction arises in a dialogue, especially in the case presented above in the dialogue between Dionysodorus and Ctesippus. Would it be at the moment when both sides of the conversation say opposite statements about the same thing; or would it be when the participants in the conversation don't say the same thing; or when neither of them mentions the thing; or would it be when one person says something and the other doesn't even talk about it; or finally, when someone says one thing and the other says something else? Faced with this complex chain of questions, I can see that contradiction will arise when the participants in a conversation give the same statement different meanings, thus creating a new idea through the same thing.

The sophists' explanations put their reputation more and more at stake in the face of Socrates' questions, because when it comes to the sophists' wise and well-crafted arguments, Socrates and his friends doubt whether these speeches were truly endowed with great virtue, as the brothers had previously claimed. Thus, the brothers find themselves caught up in a series of contradictions in which they become the victims, no longer the authors and creators of the contradictions, and a cycle begins in the book in which the Sophists refuse to answer and demand answers from their interlocutor.

In the third round, a new sophism arises, based on homonymy, to try to overthrow Socrates; thus, the brothers engage in an intense discussion about the *noounta* (things they perceive/things they mean), being surprised by Socrates who concludes that the arguments used by the sophist brothers:

"remains in the same place and still, as before, having knocked down the adversary, falls, and that the way not to be subject to this has not yet been found by your art; and this, since it is so admirable with regard to the precision of words."[55] .

Thus, once again, the question of the qualification of words within a dialogue draws attention to the significant distinction between eristics and dialectics[56] .

Finally, after so many attempts to get the Sophist brothers to demonstrate their knowledge, Socrates, in order to prevent Ctesippus from losing his temper, concluded that the brothers were not willing to explain themselves seriously, but were rather "baffling us with their magician's tricks"[57] . However, because the art of the sophists impressed Socrates and he was amazed by the virtue of his brothers, he begged, pleaded and encouraged Euthydemus and Dionysodorus to show him and his friends the way in a serious way. And this is precisely linked to the idea that the quality involved in

---

55 *Eutidemo*, 288.
56 KERFERD, 2003, p.18.
57 *Euthydemus*, 288c.

the possession of an art or knowledge implies the correct or incorrect use that can be made of a given art. As Socrates says: "If you direct them with ignorance, they are worse evils than their opposites, all the more capable of serving the one who directs them, who is evil"[58] .

Thus, in the sequence of the Socratic *epideixis, there is* the search for science, and Socrates demonstrates that it is necessary to cultivate knowledge, because through this we will be acquiring a science, with the proviso that all science will be of good use if we know how to use it properly. Socrates concludes that what is needed is a science in which both the production and the knowledge of how to use what it produces coincide.

Faced with this, Socrates asks the following question: "If we were to learn the art of producing speeches - is this what we would need to acquire in order to be happy?"[59] . Clinias disagrees and bases his idea on the fact that the act of producing a speech is distinct from the art of using it, stating that the art of producing speeches is not the one whose acquisition would bring happiness. Socrates believed that the art of the general is an art capable of acquiring happiness, which is once again contested by Clinias, who says that they have the gift of "capturing" something, but not of making use of it.

Based on this reflection, Clinias mentions that geometers, astronomers and calculators are hunters who don't produce, but discover the figures that they are, that is, not knowing how to use them themselves, they hand over their discoveries to the dialecticians, thus highlighting yet another striking characteristic of Plato's disciples with regard to the infinite search for truth. Thus, the dialecticians, as Clinias mentions, aim to counter arguments and derive new ideas from them that prove what is being said, but this is done through a rational investigation in which the opposition of conflicting elements and the understanding of the role of these elements, In other words, from the moment a "discovery" is handed over to the dialecticians, they contextualize this object in such a way as to confront everything that is given as absolute truth by relating it to other realities and theories in order to reach a plausible conclusion with a common goal.

After the dialogue between Socrates and Criton, the philosopher asks the Sophists for help to get out of the aporia (uncertainty or hesitation about what one wants to say), thus leading to the Eristic *epideixis,* exposing the principle of non-contradiction in the Sophistic fashion. What Socrates was looking for was a beautiful science that would make him happy for the rest of his life, and the Sophist brothers were seen by him as the link to this discovery. In trying to demonstrate the art of persuasion to Socrates, we can see the role of contradiction in the sophists' speeches, since the

58 *Euthydemus,* 281d.
59 *Euthydemus,* 289c.

moment they demonstrate that man can be wise and not wise at the same time, they ratify that we can have relatively different understandings of the same thing, thus extracting contradiction in its densest form. We can see here that this is the principle of contradiction being defended by the Sophists, and thus portrays a principle that states that a thing can be and not be at the same time.

Therefore, faced with the understanding that it is impossible for the same thing to be and not be at the same time, the Sophists affirmed that the moment you know one thing, you will know absolutely everything, because "there cannot be someone who knows and someone who doesn't know at the same time"[60] . Thus, through their art of contradiction, the sophists were messing with the philosophers' heads in Eristic fashion.

At this point we are faced with skeptical behavior on the part of the anti-sophists. The mere fact that the brothers claimed to possess the wisdom of all things did not convince them; therefore, Ctesippus asked them to prove it, demonstrating once again the immense difference between eristics and dialectics [61] . The first deals with something concrete in terms of its existence and the meaning of things, demonstrating an ideal that must be duly justified and based on something solid capable of providing plausible explanations, showing the elements on which they are based. On the other hand, we have eristics, the art of "anything is possible" - you just have to say it, so there's no need to prove anything, just argue and persuade the other person that you're telling the truth. Thus, the sophists remained unyielding when they claimed to know all things and, to the surprise of many, there were no questions that they didn't answer, even the most inconvenient ones.

Another point worth highlighting is the fact that Socrates says that he knows things through his soul, showing that the quest for knowledge has in its path the incessant search for a truth composed of essence, with an end end endowed with meaning; in this way, dialectics always prevails over eristics for Socrates, but he is incapable of seeing this distinction clearly, because he doesn't know that the wordplay preached by the sophists is a totally opposite branch to that preached by Plato's disciples.

Socrates raises a problem: how can you say that you know something that isn't true? This question illustrates the main aim of dialectic, the aim of finding the truth. Caught in a contradiction, the sophist deflects the issue with a string of arguments in a dialogue between Socrates and Dionysodorus. So Socrates says:

[...] Well, Dionisodorus, I said, the best thing for me is to answer you. Because, I'm afraid, you're not going to stop asking questions, I'm almost certain of it, with ill will towards me and creating obstacles, so that

60 *Euthydemus,* 294.
61KERFERD, 2003, p. 18.

Euthydemus doesn't teach me that wise thing[62] .

Faced with this, the nonsense continues, beyond homonymy and ignorance of the relationship, and Ctesippus enters the scene with brilliant tirades, as Plato observes in his work. As the tussle continues between Ctesippus and the Sophist brothers, arguments arise based on the ambiguity of syntax, i.e. they begin to discuss the arrangement of words in a sentence and the logic between them[63] .

Faced with all the arguments put forward by the sophists, at the moment when a discussion opens up about which Gods are sacred to Socrates, there is a strong questioning with imminent statements that will overthrow even the most congenital beliefs. Thus, when asked if Socrates had a "paternal Zeus" [64] , the latter, about to fall into a brilliant trap set by the sophists, replied that he didn't, but that he did have altars and sacred rituals, like Apollo and Athena. After this statement, their fallacies end with the following passage:

So these would be your gods, wouldn't they?" he said. - Ancestral gods, I said, and masters. - In any case, they're yours," he said. Or didn't you agree that they were yours? - I agreed, I said. Otherwise, what will become of me? - So, he said, are these gods animals too? Because you agreed that all things that have a soul are animals. Or don't these gods have souls? -Yes, I said. - So they're animals too? - They are animals, I said. - And among the animals, he said, you agreed that all those you can give, sell and sacrifice to the god you want are yours. - I agreed, I said. Well, I can't make a retraction, Euthydemus. - Come on, tell me, he said. Since you agree that Zeus and all the other gods are yours, is it possible for you to sell them or give them away or use them in any other way you want, like the other animals?[65] .

Faced with this complex discourse in which the contexts considered sanctified by the philosophers are questioned, Socrates and Ctesippus give up and conclude that the reduction of the opponents silences them, marking the victory of the Sophists, who are seen as unbeatable men with formidable speeches and arguments. At this point, there is nothing to say other than to praise the spectacular contexts of the two men surrounded by applause from those present who were delighted by the splendid demonstration of the art of contradiction.

3.3. Partial Conclusion

After so many "battles" of dialog and argument, we are faced with a valuable art in which the sophists' skills are not properly known, often being misrepresented as scammers, leaving aside the beauty and grandeur of eristics. However, it is an art that must be used seriously and the brothers themselves contribute to this art, which can be extremely useful in court, becoming an art that is

---

62 *Eutidemo*, 298e.
63 ETIM gr. *súntaksis,eôs* 'organization, composition; treatise; grammatical construction'
64*Eutidemo*, 302d.
65*Euthydemus*, 302e/ 303.

spent every moment of the day playing at refuting others for fun and games. Therefore, if you look at these skills differently, you can see that they are egalitarian in the sense that anyone who is daring and able to learn and pay for these teachings can practice this art, as Socrates concludes in this passage:

they say that they are able to teach anyone who is willing to give them money and that they do not exclude any natural inclination or age and that, above all, it is good for you to hear that not even being in business absolutely prevents anyone from easily learning their knowledge[66].

There's also the fact that when you argue something:

[...] you sew men's mouths shut, as you also say; but because it's not only other people's mouths, but also your own, it's very kind, and it takes away what's unbearable about arguments[67].

Thus, you don't win an argument with empty arguments, but with the strength of your arguments curtailed by the unique impact and brilliance of the sophists.

The last considerations take place between Socrates and Criton regarding the difficult distinction between philosophy, rhetoric, eristica and politics. Thus, Plato ends the work by leading us to a series of reflections and a question in the sense of, are the sophists villains or good guys? What exactly Plato is trying to convey is a negative side to the activities of sophists who are just playing around, labeled in a way in which the search for truth will always be the priority, being an essential element. However, the moment the eristica run away from such guidelines and end up becoming the refuters of everything and everyone, they are seen as falsifiers, surrounded by contradictory speeches based on appearances and opinions that are often far removed from reality.

In this way, Plato maintains that eristica is the art of inventing contradictions[68], which cannot be categorized in an unequivocal way because it portrays real wisdom, where the arguments are plausible and based on the intelligence and expertise inherent in the sophists who are dedicated and shrewd in the creation and defense of their speeches. And this is especially useful for the public sphere of the Courts that are emerging in Greece.

The importance of practicing an art in a good and correct way, in other words, in an appropriate and coherent way, is essential in our study. When we are dealing with an art such as eristics, which can influence us in so many ways, it is essential that it is practiced as carefully as possible. Thus, based on Socrates' statement about the correct use of goods, it is possible to compare it with the good use of the sophists' art. For, just as it is necessary to make good use of goods in order to extract the best benefit from them, it is vital that the same applies to the art of refutation, because if a man possesses

66 *Euthydemus*, 304b.
67 *Euthydemus*, 303e.
68 KERFERD, 2003.

the gift of counter-arguing any opponent, but uses this virtue to degrade and shame the other, it ceases to be something great and becomes something meaningless.

In this way, just as Socrates argues that wisdom is the greatest good of all, it is necessary to be wise in order to manage the benefits provided by the good use of goods. In the same way, I say that having the art of persuasion and using it with ignorance will bring greater harm than if you didn't have this gift, because if you practice a technique with wisdom and prudence, using serious and correct methods, it is possible to extract the best that man can be as a person, that is, it is possible to grow as a being through the good use of the technique.

Thus, it is not enough to possess the technique of eristics; it is essential to act in a way that goes against the practice of the sophist brothers who abuse their gift by using it unequivocally and without seriousness. Given this analysis, it is possible to understand the criticism leveled by Plato, who criticizes this kind of unscrupulous and arrogant sophist, who misuses eristics and paints a false image of all the other sophists. In this way, Plato doesn't criticize the entire class of sophists, but rather those considered to be bad sophists who use and practice this art in the wrong way, even though they had everything to practice it correctly.

Based on this difference between the bad and the good use of eristics, a good example is the way in which the brothers Euthydemus and Dionysodorus take advantage of this technique, in line with the brilliant way in which Antiphon acts. From this point of view, we see sophists who have totally different objectives, even though they come from the same class of thinkers and practice the same art, each in their own way, applying their gift in a peculiar way. While the brothers don't make good use of this art, proving to be a kind of bad sophist, we have Antiphon, who is an admirable sage who creates persuasive speeches with credible content and, above all, extracts the best that eristics has to offer.

CONCLUSION

The formation of a city dates back to the beginning of the world, because it reflects the culture of the people who started an organized society with ethical and moral values. There is a whole tradition that should be followed and passed on from the elders to the young, in order to preserve the ancestors and continue to build a society that is conscious and capable of forming good citizens. The setting chosen for our study was the city of Athens, surrounded by the most varied types of philosophers who portrayed each one's conception of the proper way to form a city. The Athenians have always prided themselves on the fact that their city was considered to be a place that allowed more freedom of speech than any other place[69] , because their speeches in the public square, the power of rhetoric and their beautiful speeches are famous all over the world.

But this story is not just about sumptuous episodes; there have been a series of attacks on thinkers considered inappropriate and even accusations of proclaiming against the sacred. However, this whole cycle only illustrates what was said earlier: when the aim is to build a city, any thought that is considered "dangerous" or out of line is seen as a risk, or even as going against what was preached so vigorously by the so-called mentors of the time. There were direct attacks that sought significant changes and transformations in favor of improvements.

Therefore, when we look at the question of the formation of cities from Plato's point of view, and also from the point of view of the Sophists, we have to pay attention to the fact that the Sophists were often considered rebellious, because for many they confronted what was essential for a virtuous society. On the other hand, in *Euthydemus we see the* need to seek, through truth, a way of acting that is more and more in line with what is preached, through the cultivation of wisdom.

The sophists were seen by many as educators who were gifted in the art of rhetoric, thus they would have been encyclopedists or enlighteners in Greece[70] . One of the main functions given to the sophists was in relation to political virtue, or rather, the means to be used in order to be successful in this field. When a sophist was sought out, it was in order to become capable of giving speeches, presenting them to the public by means of eloquent and convincing speeches. Thus, by paying these thinkers, it was possible to take lessons and become one of them.

From the way the Sophists organized themselves, along with their teaching methods, it became possible to reflect on their students their arguments with their unpredictable and inconclusive effect in the face of opposing arguments. It is certainly important to mention the fact that the interaction between teacher and student was seen as part of the learning process, allowing through this living

---

69 KERFERD, 2003, p. 40.
70 Ibid, p. 23

together, not only an intimate contact with the mind and personality of the sophists, but also with the intellectual stimulus of the association of one with the other[71] .

With regard to teaching methods, the first stage was to select the topic to be debated and then rhetorical exercises would be carried out on that subject, as if it were a simulation of what would be done in the courts and assemblies.

For Antiphon, the formation of the city would be based on mechanisms that made people think, so that through the schematic models of speeches he drew up, he would be able to extract something from the citizen that might be hidden inside him, but when he described certain situations, he would be able to study and imitate them in order to act correctly. In other words, through his speeches where he presents the view from both sides, he would demonstrate responsibility, notions of safety and good conduct, among other good behaviors. In this sense, Antiphon would be presenting a good use of the art of refutation that goes hand in hand with the good use that philosophy argues exists in the art of dialectic.

The fact is that through his schemes he gives the idea of different situations, where you could position yourself for the prosecution or the defense; but above all, he seeks to show the students who would make up the core of society at the time the examples to be followed or not, presenting them with both sides of the coin.

A good example is the *Tetralogy* in which a boy is accidentally hit by a javelin while watching a competition in a gymnasium. This event demonstrates how the prosecution and the defense act in such a case and raises the issue of responsibility, both for the person responsible for throwing the javelin and for the spectators. By countering each other's arguments, the students' minds are formed with notions of conduct, allowing them to become great orators and, in turn, great citizens.

An analysis of the work *Euthydemus shows* that the entire dialogue seeks to lead the young Clinias along the path of wisdom and virtue, since only in this way would he become a dignified man, thus emerging as a true citizen. It can be seen that in both works it was not enough to form a city, but rather to form a city made up of decent people with unblemished conduct and character; however, what we see are different mechanisms for this. While for Plato it was necessary to form cities with citizens who reflected men of integrity, who should seek the truth above all on the basis of real experiences that would be able to prove everything that would be said; on the other hand, we have the sophists, who allowed men to learn their techniques, enriching their minds with methods that would make them prepared to face any argument, not based on absolute truth, but on a truth relative to the process in court.

71 Ibid, p.55.

There are two aspects in which Antiphon's *Tetralogies are* related to *Euthydemus*, the dialogue written by Plato. The first is that the work of the sophist Antiphon and the work of Plato, however distinct they may be, because each belongs to a "species" of thinker, and there is a certain rivalry between them, which can exhibit certain similarities when seen from a different perspective, take on new shapes because they are seen from the perspective of contradiction.

Thus an important question arises regarding the methods used by the sophists and the philosophers: if the sophists are seen by the philosophers as men who misuse the method of refutation, it is because they, as men who use the same method, have concluded the correct way and the incorrect way of doing so. In other words, if philosophers like Plato are so critical of the method of refutation used by the Sophists that they vigorously claim that they use it incorrectly, it is because philosophers, having the same method, feel obliged to warn about the good or bad use of a technique that is also used by them, in particular, the concept of refutation. Therefore, the equipollence of discourse is something common to both thinkers, what oscillates is the purpose of what is sought, that is, the objective. While on the one hand we have philosophers who are determined to seek the truth, on the other there are sophists who aim to win the discourse through the strongest counter-argument. Thus we have the greatest distinction between these two classes of thinkers in terms of the measures used to achieve this "victory", that is, the philosophers refuse to argue at any price, unlike the sophists who are more audacious, this being Plato's greatest criticism of the sophists.

The relativism of the brothers and their ambition to win all the speeches, regardless of what they are defending, is something that differentiates them from the sophist Antiphon, because, contrary to what is thought of the sophists, they were not a sect or school, but a profession that did not have a doctrinal community[72] . Therefore, if one sophist behaved in a questionable way, he couldn't drag the others down with him, because you can't condemn the whole because of the mistakes of a few.

Thus, it can be seen that although the Sophist brothers and Antiphon belong to the same class of thinkers, they differ immensely. On the one hand we have the brothers with their convinced, relentless and playful relativism, and on the other hand we have Antiphon, called the "cook of speeches"[73] , who through his power of disparity constructed speeches that were different in content and form. Antiphon stands out because he was not a sophist who aimed to win every debate at any price, nor did he intend to be a relativist. When we turn our attention to Antiphon, we come across a skillful and elegant sophist who, through the verisimilitude of his speeches, plausibly and seriously demonstrates how it is to reverse the poles of an action, that is, to go from the condition of

72 KERFERD, 2003, p. 20.
73 ANTIFONTE, 2008, p. 8.

innocent victim to defendant, just as it is possible to absolve the guilt of the accused.[74]

Antiphon's skill was so insightful that he had a kind of consulting room where he would ask and answer questions of the sick, encouraging them with his words so that they could get rid of their afflictions. It is thus clear that Aniphon, as a sophist, had the ability to create arguments that could be molded to each specific case, so that when he needed to produce speeches, he would do so in the same way. This statement corroborates the *tetralogies*, in which the philosopher contradicts himself, carrying out rhetorical exercises that make him able to speak and overthrow any speech.

When drawing a parallel between two works that represent such different contents, it becomes a little complicated to know how far we can go with such a comparison, since when we approach these works, we are faced with a universe of issues that do not necessarily dialog with each other. Although in terms of content there is no objective dialogue, in terms of the method of contradiction there is a lot in common. The Platonic dialogue shows a critical version of the Sophists' method, but it's important to question whether Antiphon himself is as inveterate a contradictor as Dionysodorus and Euthydemus seem to be. It seems to us that Antiphon makes good use of his method and that he wouldn't be willing to go out refuting people just for the sake of refuting and winning any clash. Antiphon's aim was to win the legal debates and present, through contradiction, some truth that emerged from the common content of the cases.

The inability to contradict oneself is another point that draws attention, because comparing these two greats shows how this art is faced in a unique way by each of these thinkers. Thus, it is possible to see that the different ways of thinking of these philosophers are crucial points in their development as people, and that this issue is a key point in defining how different people will argue, contradict and persuade.

In this case, using as examples the characters described in *Euthydemus* and the philosopher Antiphon in his work *Testimonies, Fragments, Speeches. We can see* that by analyzing the points proposed in this study, we are witnessing the birth of contradiction in different situations. This makes it possible for this phenomenon to become more visible in circumstances that often go unnoticed, but which represent great advances for an entire generation.

It's important to note that when we start studying Contradiction, we come across different methods by which this phenomenon occurs. We can see it from the point of view of Plato's followers through a dialectical approach, which is difficult to characterize in detail, but strongly tends to mean "the ideal method, whatever it may be"[75] , as long as it is something firm and unchanging, with objects of a similar nature. On the other hand, we have the sophists' eristics as a rich argumentative

74 SILVA, 2014.
75 KERFERD, 2003, p. 113.

technique, capable of changing the way things appear to be, giving a certain thing a different importance, depending on the intention of the speaker.

So, on the one hand, we have Plato, who seeks the truth, which is real knowledge and must seek permanent entities that are secure and reliable, in order to guarantee absolute truth. On the other hand, the sophists were seen as instructors in wisdom and virtue, because they were able to elevate half-truths to a whole truth, capable of overturning any argument raised. They gained listeners who appreciated the effect that the contradictory arguments put forward by the sophists were able to have on their opponents.

At this point, it is important to emphasize how the proper use of the technique called eristics was fundamental in this process. For the art of refutation requires a serious and plausible stance, because, unlike the sophist brothers who practiced this technique without prudence and with jokes, the sophistical method was something remarkable in the history of philosophy. Thus, when refuting arguments it is necessary to steer clear of games that lead the "opponent" into error, compromising a good dialogue with jokes and ambiguous insinuations. In order to make good use of the refutation method, it is enough to act in an attentive and fair manner, understanding what the other person is saying and refuting it with strong and acceptable arguments that win over the other person through your ability to contradict and not through cheating.

The ability to contradict is the gift of few, because those who mastered this method didn't opt for long or short speeches, but for moderate ones, surrounded by words that made people disbelieve in what was true. Therefore, the sophists were able to express that everything they said was the best it could be, in other words, they were the wisest and most plausible arguments for a defense.

In this way, when we compare what is described in *Euthydemus* with the work of Antiphon, we have on the one hand thinkers who proceed by negations, because at every step taken in a research it is necessary to be sure whether something is true or false, so that in the end everything that is true is extracted; and on the other hand, a clever and original thinker, who has such contradictory arguments that one wonders if they were two different thinkers or just one who was able to defend ideas from the left and the right, with the same brilliance and genius in both.

In short, we can see how contradiction has this purpose because it takes us out of our comfort zone by putting into play beliefs that we vigorously defend, causing an "internal storm", like confusion, which leads us to navigate new ideas and worlds, completely drowning out later thoughts; or, on the contrary, having a totally different effect, causing the complete devastation of any new or future considerations, ratifying prejudices inherent in our mind, and therefore requiring nothing more to be added or modified. I understand contradiction as a kind of "little parasite", because it causes confusion in our most concrete thoughts.

Thus, when we look at issues that seem irrelevant, but are treated differently by these thinkers, we are presented with the phenomenon of contradiction, allowing us to see two important authors relating in an involuntary way, but which leads to great discoveries, due to the greatness involved in the difference of their thoughts.

BIBLIOGRAPHICAL REFERENCES

MAIN BIBLIOGRAPHY

ANTIFONTE. *Testimonies, fragments, speeches.* Translated by Luis Felipe Bellintani Ribeiro. Luis Felipe Bellintani Ribeiro. Sao Paulo: Ediçoes Loyola, 2008.

PLATO. *Euthydemus.* Text established and annotated by John Burnet. Trad. Maura Inglésias. Rio de Janeiro: Ed. PUC-Rio, Loyola, 2011.

SECONDARY BIBLIOGRAPHY

ARAÙJO, C. *Da Arte - a reading of Plato's Gorgias.* Belo Horizonte: Ed. UFMG, 2008.

BILLIER, Jean-Cassien, MARYIOLI, Hàgale. History of the Philosophy of Law. Trad. Mauricio de Andrade. Sao Paulo: Manole, 2005.

CASERTANO, G. *Sophist.* Sao Paulo: Paulus, 2010.

CASSIN, Barbara. The Sophistic Effect, philosophy, rhetoric, literature. Trad. Ana Lùcia de Oliveira, Maria Cristina Franco Ferraz and Paulo Pinheiro. Sao Paulo: Ed. 34, 2005.

GRAÇA, José Augusto Ribeiro Antifonte e o movimento sofista : trabalho de sintese / Jose Augusto Caiado Ribeiro Graca.- [Porto] : [Ediçao do Autor], 1993-1994.

KERFERD, G.B. The Sophist Movement. Trad. Margarida Oliva. Loyola Publications, 2003.

MARQUES, Marcelo P. (Org.) Theories of the image in antiquity. Sao Paulo: Paulus Ed., 2012.

MURCHO, Desidèrio. What is a Law of Nature?.   Available

at: <http://dererummundi.blogspot.com.br/2007/04/o-que-uma-lei-da-natureza.html>.

RIBEIRO, L. F. B. A Multiple Antiphon. In Annals of Classical Philosophy, 2008.

Accessed on: Oct. 12

SILVA, Anna. Persuasion and responsibility: itineraries of a tragic and philosophical epic in Antiphon. Thesis (doctorate) Universidade Federal de Minas Gerais, Faculdade Filosofia e Ciências Humanas, 2014.

I want morebooks!

Buy your books fast and straightforward online - at one of world's fastest growing online book stores! Environmentally sound due to Print-on-Demand technologies.

Buy your books online at
www.morebooks.shop

Kaufen Sie Ihre Bücher schnell und unkompliziert online – auf einer der am schnellsten wachsenden Buchhandelsplattformen weltweit! Dank Print-On-Demand umwelt- und ressourcenschonend produziert.

Bücher schneller online kaufen
www.morebooks.shop

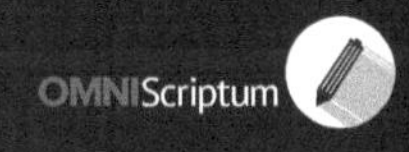

Printed by Books on Demand GmbH, Norderstedt / Germany